HEAVEN

HEAVEN

by

Frank Townshend

THE BOOK TREE
San Diego, California

originally published 1930
Alfred A. Knopf, Inc.
New York

All new material & revisions
© 2018 The Book Tree
All rights reserved

ISBN 978-1-58509-374-8

Cover layout
Paul Tice

Cover Art
©
PHOTOCREO
Michael Bednarek

Published by
The Book Tree
P.O. Box 16476
San Diego, CA 92176
www.thebooktree.com

We provide fascinating and educational products to help awaken the public to new ideas and information that would not be available otherwise.
Call 1 (800) 700-8733 for our *FREE BOOK TREE CATALOG*.

TO
ALEXEY D'ORMESSON

In the Universe live I.
In my heart
Lives Heaven.

CONTENTS

		Page
I.	THE KINGDOM OF HEAVEN	3
II.	GOD	61
III.	ETERNAL LIFE	71

HEAVEN

THE KINGDOM OF HEAVEN

1

AFTER a long journey
I came to the Gates of Heaven.

2

THE keeper of the outer gate said:
I suppose you have come to see God.
I answered:
No — I have come to stay.
Whereupon the outer gate was opened.

The keeper of the inner gate said:
What have you brought?
I answered:
Myself.
Whereupon the inner gate was opened.

The keeper of the innermost gate said:
What do you want?
I answered:
To love — to understand — to do.
And immediately the innermost gate stood open.

3

WITHIN the innermost gate there was a Customs-house;
And inside the Customs-house an Officer handed me this list of Prohibited Articles:

Hopes, Fears, Desires
(Excepting a reasonable amount of personal and bodily desires).
Respectability, Superiority, Flatulence.
Motives (conscious or unconscious).
Regrets.
Pet Schemes and Fancy Theories.
Pride (real or artificial).
High Purposes and Benevolent Designs.
Cleverness, Reputation, Complaints.
Beliefs, Pretensions, Ideals, Arrangements, Habits.
Attitudes, Poses, Modesty.
Virtues, Vices, Shame.
Ambitions (worldly or unworldly).
Fixed Opinions (orthodox or unorthodox).
Standards.
Illusions.

I swore that I had none of the above.

4

IN a general way, the Customs Officer explained,
You may not bring anything in here except yourself;
And even that has to be purged of all dross.

THE KINGDOM OF HEAVEN

I answered:
But I can bring in some bodily desires?

He looked at me as if he thought I was a fool.
Then he said:
You can't come in here without a body;
And you can't have a body that has no bodily needs;
Unless yours is made of cardboard.

I thought of saying that I would report him for impertinence.
Then I remembered what I had sworn,
And went on.

5

AFTER all, it was not altogether his fault.
For from time immemorial the customs authorities had officially forbidden the bringing in of bodily desires.
And though for the most part they had shut their eyes to the importing of a reasonable amount,
It was only recently that they had officially recognized its necessity.

Small wonder, then, that large numbers of people should wish to reassure themselves about so important a matter,
To the irritation of the customs officials.

6

BUT I laughed to myself when I thought of what my friends would say

When they heard that I could get in here with my pagan
    body,
My virtues left outside.

7

WHEN I came out of the Customs-house,
I found myself on the top of a hill.
Before me there stretched a lawn;
And beyond it, a group of buildings.

8

THE first was a magnificent structure called:
The Court of Discarded Symbols.

Inside there was a collection of Symbols, arranged in order,
Beginning with the most modern, and reaching back to the
    dawn of history and beyond.

Near the entrance were the latest tanks and battle-ships,
Which were regarded as Symbols of power,
And sometimes of peace.
And there were expensive motor-cars and yachts,
Which were symbolical of wealth.
Further on I saw the flags of all the nations,
And a collection of machines,
Symbols of efficiency.

There were orders and decorations and diplomas,
Crowns and sceptres.

THE KINGDOM OF HEAVEN

Symbols of marriage and of mourning — of virginity and vaccination.
Balance-sheets and crests and keys.
And clothes, which were Symbols of respectability,
Or of servitude.
Among them I noticed an Emperor's birthday robe,
Embroidered all over with long life and happiness;
And a pair of plain black trousers,
Belonging to a former President;
And a sacred hat-box from the East.

9

Half-way through the building, I went up into a gallery, where there was a collection of Ceremonies, without their Symbols,
The Symbols being kept in the hall below.

There I saw marriages without rings or orange-blossom;
Funerals without paper tabernacles or fireworks;
And religious services without chalices or croziers or gilded fish.

10

Further on a King was being crowned without any crown;
And the King himself looked palely emblematic.

I noticed that the High Priest who officiated was clothed only in his underwear
(By a well-known maker).

[7]

HEAVEN:

For the rest of his robes, being symbolic,
Were kept in the hall below.

I said to the High Priest:
If your underclothing had been the Symbol of anything —
Purity, for instance —
You would be naked like me.
But he appeared not to hear.

II

BACK in the main hall, I passed by Symbols of ever increasing antiquity;
Scales, swords, helmets;
White and black horses — maidens and first-borns;
Dragons, dragon-killers, heroes;
Bulls and snakes;
Symbols of sacrifice and of safety;
The Cross, the sacred Bo-tree, the Lotus;
Cup and spear;
The Moon and the Sun.

I said to the attendant:
Most of these look hollow.
That depends, he answered;
Once they were full of life,
The livest things imaginable.

And on I went past all the Symbols the world has ever known,

Until I came at last to the Universal Egg
Floating in water.

I turned it inside out.
That was that;
But I was surprised to find myself inside.

12

As I went out, the attendant handed me a card on which was printed:
Warning.
Visitors are warned that it is dangerous to proceed without taking a Symbol.
On the other hand, visitors who overburden themselves with Symbols will be unable to proceed far.

I said:
Well, that is just the sensible sort of thing that I was always being told on Earth.
He answered:
As a matter of fact, you will be taking a Symbol with you without knowing it.
You will be able to get rid of it later on, which will be quite all right.

With this cryptic remark,
He bowed me out.

13

The next building was called:
The House of Madness.

On the walls of the entrance hall there were cross-sections of every imaginable type of mind,
Normal and abnormal,
In every conceivable mood.

14

THE main room bore a striking resemblance to an operating-theatre.

In the middle, on a glass-topped table,
There was laid out for inspection
My own mind.

It disconcerted me for a moment to see my own mind in such unusual surroundings;
But after a little while I was able to look at it working.

And I saw all my own thoughts;
Observing how they stretched forth to the uttermost parts of the Earth,
Including all that there was on Earth,
And had ever been.

And how that they reached beyond the Earth, and encompassed the Universe.
And how that they reflected everything.

At last I dared to adventure with it;
To expose it to all sorts of experiences.

THE KINGDOM OF HEAVEN

15

SUDDENLY I saw myself arriving,
In a very handsome motor-car,
At the Hall of Fantasy,
Where one could be anything one liked.

There were young gentlemen who fancied themselves as
    dictators;
Maids — who fancied noble lovers,
Every sort of Utopia.
And it was there that people wove desirable characters
In which to clothe the objects of their affection.

16

THERE I became a Prime Minister;
And for every battle-ship I launched,
I shed a genuine tear
Upon
An Unknown Soldier's Tomb.

Then I became a King
Bestowing decorations
(Costing fourteen shillings each),
With such magnificence
As to vibrate.

After which I became a dancer,
With the most beautiful body that ever was;

And while a million eyes were watching me,
I lived a dance.

Last of all I became a Bishop,
Floating down the aisle,
Feeling like God.

17

I was so intrigued that it was only by summoning the utmost
 energy and determination that I got out and on to the
 next building:
The Palace of Ease and Perfect Comfort.

18

The Palace of Ease and Perfect Comfort
Was full of beds and settled incomes.
And there were supplies of hope and forgetfulness and rage
(The last for people who found it comforting to lose their
 tempers);
And of suicide.

Here too were some of the best clubs and houses and hotels,
Together with bankers and politicians and other suppliers
 of Security.
And beyond them all — the shadowy form of the Universal
 Mother,
Beckoning me back to peace and irresponsibility.

THE KINGDOM OF HEAVEN

19

I STOOD in the middle and shouted:
No.
A thousand times — No.
I will come here when I want a little rest,
But I'm damned if I'll be ensnared by this.
And I shouted again,
A thousand times — No.

Then it seemed that all the club secretaries and hotel managers,
And bankers and politicians and sellers of balloon tires,
And other purveyors of Ease and Safety,
Rose up
And got me out.

20

OUTSIDE I met a little old lady in black,
Who said:
Have you visited the Palace of Unfulfilled Desire?
It is full of fornication and other deadly sins.
I answered:
Surely I met you in the Court of Discarded Symbols?
Upon which she promptly disappeared,
And I went into the Palace of Unfulfilled Desire.

21

THERE were things there that publishers will not publish,
But which readers like to read about.

Yet there was nothing that I did not know,
Or had not done.
Nor anything that I would not do again
If it seemed right to do.

So that I came quite easily through the Palace of Unfulfilled
    Desire.

22

For a little while I followed a path
Marked: Path of Endurance.
It led me straight up to an austere-looking building labelled:
Department of Neglected Duties.

23

The vestibule was full of the beautiful expressions
Of those who had done theirs.
And as I walked through the main hall, every kind of Duty
    beckoned to me,
Striking alluring attitudes.

There was my Duty to my God, and to my King, and to my
    Fatherland.
There was my Duty to society, to my parents, to my family,
    and to myself.
My Duty to a certain night-club,
Of which I was once a member.
And my Duty, gentle reader,
To you.

Further on were a number of shining examples,
Which I thought would have looked better
If they had not been so highly polished.

24

As I went out, I passed through a room containing a collection of Missed Opportunities,
Who crowded round me, seeking recognition.

I said to them:
Look here,
Whenever one of you presented himself to me,
I did whatever it was in my heart to do.
And now you are only here
To provide one Final Opportunity
For self-pity;
To which I also give a miss.

25

I came next to the Hall of Benevolent Designs.

The first room was devoted to Idealism,
And was so crowded with Good Works
That I had some difficulty in getting through.

26

Inside was an enormous hall in which were stalls for every Philanthropic Society on Earth.

HEAVEN:

It was here that I came nearest to shattering my Heaven;
For I was immediately surrounded by numbers of dear old ladies, pestering me for money for missionaries.
I was so bothered and perplexed that, for a moment, I was on the point of escaping their importunities,
And at the same time satisfying my own conscience,
By giving an equally handsome subscription to the Islamic Mission in Africa,
As to the Baptist Mission in China;
When the sudden memory of the Palace of Ease and Perfect Comfort
Saved my soul.

27

As I went towards the exit, it seemed to me that the advertisements for the sale of religious books
Were altogether outdone by those concerned with the sale of drink.
While temperance societies and vegetarians
Were making more noise in proportion to their numbers
Than the venders of good taste in clothes.

I was a little surprised to see drink and clothes among the Benevolent Designs;
But there they were.

28

Out in the open, I found myself on a terrace, overlooking a lake,
Called Lake Unconscious.

THE KINGDOM OF HEAVEN

Taking a little boat,
I started to row across.

29

At first nothing unusual happened.

Then there arose out of the lake
Unexpected forms
Altering the course of my boat,
Which at times came near to being wrecked.

To make matters worse, the surface of the water was so
    rippled by the breeze
That I could not see what lay below.

30

But once, when the wind dropped,
And the ripple on the surface of the lake died away,
And the sun shone,
For an instant — I saw clearly.

And there, in the depths beneath me,
Was a whole world;
And the stars.

31

On the far side of the lake, I found myself walking up an
    avenue
Marked: To the Temple of Fame;
With statues on either side.

HEAVEN:

32

As I passed I noticed that the statues were continually being changed.
New ones were put in; old ones were taken out.
Some remained only a little while;
Others for long periods;
And some that had been taken away
Were brought back again later.

But there was not one that did not fall to pieces in the end.

33

LEADING up to the temple door was a wide staircase,
Red carpeted.
And on either side of the steps were trumpeters,
Who looked to me as if they might well have been housed
In the Court of Discarded Symbols.

34

THE Temple of Fame itself
Was rather over-heated,
And appeared to be quite empty.

Suddenly a very loud speaker began:
You are looking for Fame.
I answered:
You are wrong.
But I am exceedingly thirsty.

THE KINGDOM OF HEAVEN

Immediately I was handed a drink;
Such a refreshing drink as is only to be had in Heaven.
And somehow or other I found myself outside the Temple
  of Fame,
With the drink.

35

ALMOST without warning there descended upon me
The dark Night of Tension.

I strained my eyes to see where I was,
And groped in different directions to find my way,
And grew fearful of the approach of some unseen enemy.

It was only when I realized that I had but to await a change
  in circumstances
That the darkness turned to light.

36

JUST then I stumbled upon a little tank
Which was full of the germs of Thought.

37

FUNNY you should find this, said the guardian;
Nearly everyone misses it.
Yet it is perhaps the most important thing here.

There are millions and millions of these germs, most of
  them destined to come to nothing;

But some will have their part in changing life.
There are germs of every kind of Thought;
Of the kind that old gentlemen have in cemeteries,
Of the kind that young people blaze into being.
Thoughts that destroy — and Thoughts that create;
Of peace and of violence;
Of action and of inaction;
Of every process in existence.

It is only a small tank,
But the germs in it continually escape.
And when one of them happens upon a favourable environment,
It breeds.

Some multiply slowly and for ever;
Others rapidly;
And so, consuming their nutriment,
Die out.

But in this tank there is a never failing supply.

38

The next building was called:
The Hall of Sweet Illusions.
It was one of the largest buildings in Heaven.

39

Inside was a wonderful collection of optical and other instruments.

There was a sort of reflector that made things look respectable,
If they were old.
Only it did not work with everything.

And a pair of spectacles which made anything your enemies did
Look unpleasant and ugly,
But which gave a satisfactory appearance
To whatever you did yourself.
They were rather trying to wear.

And there were mirrors in which everyone could see everything,
From his own point of view.

40

IN the centre of the hall, in glass cases,
Were a number of Cherished Illusions;
The most popular being a Cherished Illusion about the importance of anything one might do
Or leave undone.

A near competitor was the idea that if one could only establish the right system,
All would be well.

And there was another that made cinemas and theatres seem more attractive
Than real life.

41

Near by was a peculiar state of mind
Whereby people were able to spend more money on jewellery than on housing the homeless,
Without feeling vulgar.

And a second which made one person feel vastly superior
To another.

42

Further on was a spectroscope that split events or proceedings into their component parts;
And which enabled one to observe only that component which was satisfying to oneself.

Thus, what from one point of view looked like a skyscraper
Seemed from another to be a silly waste of time,
And from a third to be a magnificent monument
To human progress.

And what from one position looked like mere obedience to orders,
Appeared from another angle to be the cowardly bombing of women and children.
While a third aspect showed the same event
As the spreading of a noble civilization.

I was amazed to see how easily those mutilated children could be made to fade out of the picture;

So that even women, who were mothers themselves,
Could approve.

43

Looking at a young lady anointing herself,
I saw that, from one point of view, she was paying a tribute to her beauty;
From another, she was spoiling her skin by robbing it of its essential natural oil;
While from a third, she was being a low-down hussy.

44

Seeing that I was interested in the instrument, the attendant explained that by inverting the prism
I could get a whole new set of subjective impressions;
Which I did.

They came out at:
Sexual lure,
Joy in disobedience to parents,
And curiosity regarding unknown toilet preparations;
The first two appearing below the conscious line.

Truly a wonderful machine.

45

Then I looked at some people making love.

46

LAST of all I looked at some worship.
I saw that, from one aspect, it was a needful help and protection to a growing race;
From another, it was cotton wool stuffed into the intelligence of the thoughtful;
While from a third, it was a beautiful and interesting ceremonial,
A survival from the past.

47

THERE was a somewhat similar apparatus for sectioning off events in Time.
By its aid a man could enjoy eating a crab,
Without any distressing picture of what the crab had eaten before;
And with no neurotic visions of what was shortly to happen to it,
When it reached the moist warm darkness of his own lower intestine.

48

BY changing the eyepiece the scale of the machine could be extended or lessened,
So that what a thousand years ago seemed like the wildest of impossibilities,
Today looked like a commonplace,
And a thousand years hence appeared childishly futile.

THE KINGDOM OF HEAVEN

There was a condenser which could be fitted to the object-glass,
Through which true things were diminished so as to have no value;
While the question of the moment,
However inane,
Loomed up into a terrific importance.

49

In the next room I saw a lens in which the whole outside world came to a focus,
To meet the focus of the inner world.

And there was a rose-coloured screen
Through which anything looked good
Provided that it showed a profit.

50

Near at hand was a pseudoscope that made it seem more desirable to be in some other place
Than the one one happened to be in;
An article of great benefit to the manufacturers of motor-cars,
And to tourist agencies.

And there was a polemoscope that gave satisfaction in talking and writing about things,
Instead of being them and doing them.

51

FURTHER on I saw a shade which cut out the present,
So that those who used it could be for ever fretting over the past,
Or glowing with the prospects of the future.

And there were head-phones through which the most banal of platitudes
Sounded like words of wisdom;
And the cheapest kinds of criticism,
Like vital thought.

52

IN an adjoining room was a microscope
Which not only prevented you from seeing anything except what you wanted to see,
But by means of which whatever you happened to be looking at
Shone out like a first and last cause.

By its aid a man who discovered the presence of some infinitesimal bug
In association with distressing circumstances,
Could destroy the bug
And keep the circumstances,
With complete satisfaction to himself.

And there were a number of coloured slides
Through which facts appeared tinted
In accord with one's mood.

THE KINGDOM OF HEAVEN

Thus — what to a critical eye looked like a dusty public square
Seemed to a tired soul
A haven of rest.

53

In the next room was an instrument which showed everything from a double point of view.
By means of it shining truth looked also like a lie;
A hotel *de luxe* — like an inferno of unhealthy labour;
Heading for destruction — like making certain of safety;
A noble profession — like a soul-destroying slavery;
Spreading false reports — like useful propaganda;
And tortured death — like heroism.

54

A similar instrument made Time simultaneous;
So that when I looked at a building,
I also saw a ruin;
When I looked at an old man — he was a little child;
And if I glanced at a soldier —
He appeared a mutilated corpse.

55

I liked best a kind of periscope, called faith,
Which enabled me to look over the walls of reasoned argument and of doubt,
And to obtain a clear view of all that lay beyond.
I do not think that there was any Illusion about it.

56

At the end of a gallery was a dark room, containing an X-ray apparatus,
Whereby one could see the inner states that had their fruition in outward acts.
By aid of it, when a man behaved like a beast in the middle of war,
I could see the beast that he kept in his heart;
And when he behaved like a fool in the middle of peace,
I could see the stupidity on which he fed his soul.

It was illuminating to watch his efforts to act like a wise angel,
While guarding the beast and the fool
In his heart.

57

Outside, under a tree,
Was a man with a telescope;
And by his side — a placard, on which was printed:
Take a Look at Earth.

So I took a look at Earth.

58

For a moment I thought that it was diseased.
For the part which was turned towards me, and which just then was lit up by the sun, was covered with purulent sores, called cities;

Beneath which the ground was all tubercled,
And from which an intolerable stink arose.
Also I noticed that out of the cities there poured quantities of waste matter,
Polluting the surrounding country.

59

I THOUGHT to myself:
If God should act with the intelligence of our modern scientists,
He would inject some antitoxin into the life stream of this planet,
Which would clear up these sore places,
Killing off the human bacteria which cause them;
And so, no doubt, destroy His own image.

Evidently His understanding
Is of a different order.

60

To make sure, I said to the man who owned the telescope:
Has God seen this?
He answered:
Yes.
He looks at it every day.

61

THE next building was called:
The Hall of Unfeigned Beliefs.

62

In the antechamber,
Which was dedicated to the Unvarnished Truth,
Were three statues, on temporary stands, representing Last
 Words.

The Last Word of Science,
The Last Word of Religion,
The Last Word of Philosophy.

63

They always keep changing, the guardian said;
That is why the stands are temporary.
We don't have one for Poetry, he went on,
For poets don't have to explain what they mean.
In fact, they can get away with anything,
Provided it is called a Poem.

Don't be too critical of the Last Word of Religion, he added.
She has had to change quite a lot lately, on account of the
 other two,
And she isn't used to it.
That's why she looks so bewildered.

But if you stayed here long enough, he went on,
You would find that all three have their ups and downs.
Once she had the central position;
But we are always having to change them round.

THE KINGDOM OF HEAVEN

And sometimes one of the three grows large, and the others — small.
And occasionally one almost disappears.

There's a man that comes in here
Who says that sooner or later we'll have all three on the same stand,
And that it's the poets will do it.
But he looks like a poet himself,
And may be biased.

64

THE Hall itself contained the most astonishing collection of Beliefs imaginable.

There were Beliefs in punishment, in authority, and in the established order of things.
Beliefs in the majesty of the law, and in the dignity of labour;
In the accuracy of science, and in the beauty of love;
In ceremonies, omens, ghosts, and charms.

And all alone,
Enshrined in a glass case,
I saw a Belief in morality;
Which, as the guardian explained to me,
Was rather threadbare,
Because it had so often been used as a substitute
For morality itself.

65

FURTHER on I remarked an enormous Belief in solemnity;
Under the shadow of which,
Everything had to be done decently
And in order.

While in the same cabinet with Beliefs in several brands of socialism
Was a Touching Confidence in government bonds.

66

THERE was a whole room devoted to Beliefs in fashionable cures.
Near the door were various kinds of psychoanalysis,
And there were corners set apart for light-cures and chiropractic and nature cures.

And I went back in time
Past a Belief in grafting glands and in operations for appendicitis,
Past treatments by sour milk and inoculations,
Past simples and balms,
And leeches and blood-letting and healing by fire,
To a Tremendous Trust in the mystical healing properties of dying hens.
So that the place began rather to resemble a torture chamber,
And I was glad to get back into the main building.

THE KINGDOM OF HEAVEN

67

THE next room was marked:
Sacred.
And there was a notice on the door to the effect that visitors
    were requested to leave their thoughts outside.

It's wonderful how that draws people, the guardian re-
    marked.
Most of them don't want to think.
In fact, if the authorities here thought more,
We'd have that notice all over the building.
Of course, he added,
There is nothing really to prevent your thinking anything
    you like.
Nobody will say anything.

68

IT seemed to me that the Beliefs in the sacred room
Were very badly arranged.
For, mixed up with a jumble of new-fangled Creeds,
There was a cast-iron support for orthodoxy
And a pot of spiritual grace.

While next to the last unblushing theory that
The more things you sell,
The more prosperous you become,
There stood a sacred cow.

And among a lot of mediæval Superstitions, Doctrines, and Dogma,
I found
A beautiful Faith in oil.

69

EVERYWHERE there were Gods:
Gods of every shape and size.
Some made in the image of animals and of flowers;
Some made in the image of man.

And I cannot remember a single activity,
From the cultivation of gardens
To the visiting of the sins of parents upon their little children,
That was not attributed to Him or Her or It.

70

FURTHER on I saw extensive buildings going up.

We are making room for a lot of new Beliefs, the guardian said;
A lot that's been presented and which we have to take in;
Though there are some who'd rather we refused them.
Belief in the destiny of man;
In equality, freedom, and understanding;
In conscious creative work;
In the rhythm of life.

THE KINGDOM OF HEAVEN

But, I suggested, you might have made room by clearing
    out some of the old rubbish.
He answered:
That is not the way this place has been run,
At least not up till now.
We keep things here until they are dead and rotting;
Then we throw them out,
Because we have to.

The older people like it better so;
They like to see the things they've been accustomed to;
And some of the young ones too.

Besides, he continued,
Many of the rottenest Ideas have only just come in.
There's a constant stream of them,
But they don't last long.
You'd be surprised if you knew how quickly things change
    sometimes in here;
And we get presents from all parts.

Sometimes, he mused,
Things seem to get here almost by accident;
Little Ideas, which we fit into any corner,
Which grow as time goes on;
Until at last they become the most important Belief here.

And sometimes Beliefs remain the same for hundreds of
    years,
Without any change to speak of.

Wonderful things, he concluded,
Beliefs.

71

I CAME next to the Court of Hard-boiled Conventions;
Where I saw the shape of a collar
Spoil a whole reception;
And some of the ghastly effect
Of wearing white gloves
At the wrong moment.

72

THERE I met a man who said that he represented what was
 Customary.
He explained to me all the things that I was expected to do,
And all the things that I was expected not to do.

It seemed to me that I saw in him the shadow of my own
 self;
For all that I had thought yesterday
He still thought today.

He was remarkably strong;
And it was only by the exercise of the utmost tact and
 circumspection
That I was able to do
Whatever I wanted.

The show piece in the Court was a mechanism for doing
 things
The same way as before.

THE KINGDOM OF HEAVEN

73

THE Hall of Vanished Hopes was most depressing;
Everything in it was shrouded with care.
And at first there seemed no way out.
It is true there were a number of exits,
Marked: Drink — Religion — Work, etc.
But all of them led back into the Hall.

Yet I do not think I should have survived
If it had not been for the temporary relief I obtained
By trying those exits.

74

AT last something or other persuaded me to open an insignificant-looking door,
Marked: Understanding.
To my surprise, it led out into the open.

It was only then that I remembered that I had told the keeper of the innermost gate
That I wanted to understand.

75

THEN, just when I thought I was alone,
I suddenly realized that I was among an enormous number of fellow beings,
All bent on the same errand as myself,
And who demanded an equal consideration.

I was carried along with the crowd
Towards the Palace of Cause and Effect.

76

The Palace of Cause and Effect was round, like a circus,
With an arena in the middle.
From the centre of the arena there spread out fan-wise, to the back and to the front,
An ever widening roadway.
And for each event that took place I could see the Causes coming on from every direction, and through all time,
Till they met in the event itself.
And from then on, the Effects spread out in different directions,
On down the ages.

77

Between the events and their Causes and Effects
There was a series of screens,
Of varying opacity.
Consequently, under certain conditions, one could only see the immediate Cause,
And the immediate Effect.

Thus — a man who beat a boy, and enjoyed doing it,
Had no conception of the deeper Causes which culminated in the beating;
And no idea of the ultimate Results of his action.

THE KINGDOM OF HEAVEN

Similarly, the Cause of a strike looked like a trivial incident,
    or the bungling of some negotiation;
Whereas it was rooted far back through a thousand layers,
    in the heart of man.
While the Effect of it seemed like loss and bitter hardship;
Whereas its healing and inspiring influences
Reached on to untold depths.

78

WHEN I had watched these things awhile,
I went into the arena myself.

So did you.

79

NEXT I came to a huge tent, packed with Flowers.

I passed by the Flowers of Wisdom.
Some were of great beauty, strangely coloured.
But I noticed that those which were plucked,
Soon died.

And there were some of the everlasting kind,
Apt to get dusty.

80

FURTHER on were Flowers of Virtue.

Here were sincerity, bravery, steadfastness,
Humility, honesty, thrift;

And a number of other old-fashioned Plants,
As one may see in any cottage garden.

And near to them a collection of modern Hybrids, of a more flamboyant character:
Efficiency, speed, getting-there,
Prosperity, and success.

81

THE attendant said:
Thousands of people come and admire these Blooms;
But the only way to really enjoy them
Is to cultivate them oneself.

I thanked him for his friendly hint, and went on.
For the scent of so many desirable Virtues, crowded into the same tent,
Was a little overpowering.

82

I CAME next to the Lost-Property Office.

Outside — there was a long queue of people.
Inside — there were houses, land, machines, works of art, money, men, animals.

All these, said the man in charge,
Are yours.
I answered:

THE KINGDOM OF HEAVEN

Good lord.
Now that I am on a journey, I have no need.
But when my journey is over,
I will come and take everything that I want.

83

NEAR by was the Hall of Superior Knowledge,
Crowded with people.

It was there that a professor's wife
Invited me to drink tea.

Among the guests were many who appeared to be bursting
    with Knowledge,
And others so weighed down with it
As to be of no further use.
And all I got to eat
Was a slice of Solid Learning.

84

AN inner room was devoted to Idle Curiosity.

Said the guardian:
We are expecting this place to close down.
The trouble is that it is so closely connected to Genuine
    Inquiry, which has been the father to all Science,
And of course it would be a mistake to close that down.

But here we only keep a lot of silly minor accidents,
Around which crowds collect;

And masses of useless Information, for publication in the
    daily press;
Trivialities — Gossip of every sort.

Still, he added, we shall be overhauled in time,
And then perhaps it will be our fate to get filled up with
    potted Knowledge.
Meanwhile there's nothing of great interest;
But if you are curious,
Come in.

85

Just then a second guardian said:
Don't listen to him;
He's a confirmed pessimist.
So long as valuable Discoveries get made by accident, we
    are bound to stay open.
That's all there is to it.

86

The last room was devoted to Perfect Proofs.

It was encumbered with logic — demonstrations;
And there were positive and negative Inferences,
And reductions to absurdity.

I found it all rather dry.

Being unwilling to risk another tea-party,
If I returned by the way I had come,

THE KINGDOM OF HEAVEN

I persuaded a sympathetic guardian to let me out by a side door.

Even so, I had to climb over a high wall,
Called Intellect;
Which was one of the most serious obstacles I met with
In all Heaven.

87

THE next building was called
The Palace of Sound Opinions.

88

INSIDE there were Opinions about every sort of thing,
Usually arranged in pairs of opposites,
Supported by the same Reasons.

And under a dome I saw a perfect collection of ten different
    Opinions about the origin of a war;
Each with its Justification.

89

THERE were several Certainties, or Foregone Conclusions,
So placed as to avoid spoiling the effect of each other.

And near the dark obtuseness of other people's Opinions
There shone
A luminous appreciation of my own.

90

The guardian drew my attention to the fact that the whole building was lit by artificial light.
He said:
We do everything we can to keep the light of truth out of here.
But, no matter what precautions we take,
The Opinions nearly all get falsified in time.
Besides, he confided,
Most of them look best by artificial light.

91

In the centre was the room of Current Opinions,
With factory attached.
For it appeared that everyone wanted the same Current Opinion at the same moment.
But as soon as an Opinion went out of fashion,
Only one example was kept.

92

In the factory there was a duplicating machine, which gave large majorities of people, of the same race or epoch,
The same Views.
By its aid, at any given moment, masses of individuals could be counted upon to have the same Opinions and Enthusiasms;
The few who differed seeming unpleasant to the rest.

And I noticed that the duplicator was so flexible in use
That, within quite a short time,
Contrary Opinions could be successfully inaugurated.

93

ADJOINING was a small room labelled:
Personal Opinion.
It was full of a thick mist,
Through which it was impossible to see anything clearly.

94

THE second, and by far the largest, half of the building
Was devoted to Exploded Notions,
Or Opinions that had become falsified.

The superintendent said:
If the authorities were wise, they would call the whole
 building
Bunkum,
And have done with it.
I have been here two thousand years, and hardly a single
 Opinion has come in that has not got falsified in time.
A few went straight to the Palace of Truth.

95

OUTSIDE there was a Maze, called Paradox;
Where every path that seemed right to follow
Seemed equally wrong:

Where good works held back progress,
While evil things hastened evolution:
Where missionaries and temperance workers brought desolation and crime in their train,
While war and pestilence
Turned men to truth and cleaner living.

96

For a moment I found it difficult to decide which path to follow;
Then a kind attendant, seeing my hesitation, said to me:
You are wondering which way to go.
There is no hurry;
Nor is it so difficult as it seems.
For every path eventually leads out of the Maze;
And whatever one you happen to be on
Is just as good as any other.

97

Not far off I came to the House of Excellent Motives;
Where, for a time, I followed various Motives such as — wealth, love, fame.
But either I did not catch up with the Motive which I happened to be following,
And so would have gone on chasing it for ever;
Or else I succeeded in reaching it,
And found that it was not what I wanted.

THE KINGDOM OF HEAVEN

98

AFTER some time I said to myself:
I shall never get out of this while I follow selfish Motives;
I had better try some of the unselfish ones.

And immediately the selfish Motives began to disguise themselves as unselfish.
So that, whenever I caught up with what I thought was an unselfish Motive,
I found that it was some old friend hidden under a disguise.
And even the most innocent excursions,
Taken with a hidden Motive,
Proved a revelation.

99

AT last I said to myself:
I shall never get out of this while I follow any Motive at all.
So I went straight ahead
Without bothering about the consequences.
Whereupon — I found myself outside the House of Excellent Motives.

100

I CAME next to the Court of the Eternal Present.

The attendant said:
We don't get many visitors.
Most people prefer the Courts of Yesterday or Tomorrow.

101

INSIDE, there was a collection of difficulties to be faced;
And an opportunity for the acceptance of personal responsibility,
At the Present Time.
And there was work,
And food for thought,
And a multitude of things to do.

But at each moment,
Only one thing was within reach.

102

THE Eternal Present was in a state of perpetual change.
As soon as an event came into existence and was dealt with,
It turned to something else.
And as the events changed,
I also changed.

And every event seemed to appear from nowhere,
Just at the right moment;
So that I never knew what was going to happen next.

103

THERE seemed to be several ways out;
Notably a side exit leading to the Hall of Fantasy;
And others leading back in the direction from which I had come.

THE KINGDOM OF HEAVEN

I perceived that I should get no further
Unless I faced the difficulties;

Which done,
The Court of the Eternal Present widened itself out in some inexplicable manner,
So as to include the whole of Heaven.

104

I WENT into the Cave of Fear without a light.
The fact was, there were numerous parties at work clearing out mares' nests and funk-holes;
And I thought that I should get a better view of things if I relied on their powerful search-lights,
Rather than on a smaller equipment of my own.

105

I FOUND the working parties full of enthusiasm;
Though such spectres and bogies as they had uncovered
Looked woefully unsubstantial,
And owed their preservation, I understood, to the thick layer of wholesome respect
Which lay over everything in the cave.

106

THE cave was enormous; and the great power of the lights
But accentuated the darkness that lay beyond.

HEAVEN:

There I saw, faintly lit up, the Fear of death;
And, reaching out of the shadows, the Fear of parental authority.

And I was amazed at the quantity and size of the myths
That kept flying into the light.

107

THEN I came to a long, straight tunnel,
Where darkness surrounded me;
And the object that I had in mind
Seemed like a golden orange — hung in mid air,
The only thing in view.

But I found that what I gained by virtue of only occupying myself with one idea,
I lost by stumbling over unseen obstacles;
And that it was better to learn to keep my purpose in sight,
Without having to get into a tunnel to do it.

108

THE Palace of Progress (Commerce and Industry) was divided into three wings.
And in each wing were represented different aspects of Progress.
In the first wing were gain, prosperity, values, etc.
In the second — beauty, utility, comfort, etc.
And in the third — slavery, industrial degradation, automatism, etc.

THE KINGDOM OF HEAVEN

And each wing had three floors, from which the exhibits
    could be viewed from the different points of view
Of the producer, consumer, and profit-maker.

109

SUDDENLY I heard a tremendous clatter,
The beating of drums and shouting.
Going towards it, I came to a gateway,
Over which were the words:
Amusement Park.

110

INSIDE I saw what I at first thought was a kiosk,
But which turned out to be a war memorial.

When I asked what it was for, the attendant explained
    that most people find it easier to erect war memorials,
To stand around them for a two minutes' silence occasionally,
Or even to go to the expense of leaving a wreath,
Than to weed out the causes of war
From their own hearts.

111

FURTHER on were a number of booths where people advertised fancy religions, drugs, drinks, insurances, etc.
And a matron with a trayful of mascots,
Called Legal, Military, and Medicinal.

HEAVEN:

And there were a number of girls selling a sort of rock,
 called Respectability,
Which was hard and sweet and pink.

112

NEAR at hand was a coco-nut shy,
Where one could throw mud at the images of all the things
 in oneself
Of which one disapproved.

And I met an old woman selling ecclesiastic hot-water
 bottles and orthodoxed cotton wool;
Some of which would be a comfort, she said,
For my poor little naked soul.

113

I CAME next to a side-show, labelled Torture Chamber.

Inside, there was a large room, divided by a sheet of glass.

To begin with, nothing happened,
Then wave after wave of desire began to fill my heart;
And every imaginable satisfaction took place on the other
 side of the glass,
Out of my reach.

And the impossibility of getting satisfaction stirred my
 imagination to still greater depths;
Which in turn were reflected beyond the glass,
Yet further out of reach.

THE KINGDOM OF HEAVEN

And as my desires increased,
So did my agony.

114

SUDDENLY I saw the trick of it
And began to laugh.
Whereupon I was put out.

115

CROSSING the Court of Honour,
Where there was a frame of mind
Which permitted an honourable man to do dishonourable
　　things,
In the name of religion or patriotism or duty,
I came to two twin booths, with banners,
On which were inscribed:
Soothing Dreams and Bitter Draughts.

116

IN Soothing Dreams the most notable exhibit was work.

I said wonderingly:
Work.
Work — a Soothing Dream.

The showman explained:
This is the kind of work in which you forget yourself;
Work for work's sake,

Like art for art's sake in the Immortal Art Pavilion,
Which I believe you have missed.

I must say that I thought it was rather a swindle.

117

In the booth called Bitter Draughts
Everything seemed entirely unsatisfactory.
In one part it was too hot,
In another too cold;
And I was irritated to find that what one did in the heat
    of the moment
Was not at all what one would like to have done
In cooler circumstances.

Here there was so much noise that I could not work,
There I kept on meeting people that I wanted to avoid;
And there were unpleasant tasks and boring occasions.
In addition to which,
Everything I ever hoped for was made impossible,
Every work — of no effect,
Every idea — futile.

Finally I had to watch all my friends
Going to apparent destruction
Without my being able to do anything for them.

Quite an exciting little show.

118

I came next to a copious fountain, called Propaganda.
An expensive-looking affair of moulded glass,
Illuminated by coloured lights.
There was a large crowd drinking in the waters.
I found them rather flat and insipid,
As free drinks often are.

The Cosmic Cocktails, sold in a bar near by,
Were far more satisfying.

119

Behind the bar was a great Wheel, called the Wheel of Existence.

As I began to be raised up,
I could only see the things nearest to me,
Which seemed to have the most importance.
But as I gained in height,
My view became wider and wider,
Until I could survey the whole of Life.
And I knew that if I ever got down,
I should not forget the vision that I had seen.

120

Beyond the Wheel of Existence was a Scenic Railway, called Experience,

HEAVEN:

Which whirled me through all sorts of unexpected situations.
It carried me up to the heights and down to the depths;
So that what at one moment seemed clear
Became uncertain.
And enthusiasms gave place to despair,
Energy to slackness,
Blind passion to calm decision.

I found that it was only by adapting myself to whatever Experience turned up
That I could begin to enjoy the journey.

121

At last I came out of all the noise and the racket
And climbed up a high mountain,
Called Mount Meditation.

122

Then, when I looked again over the Courts of Heaven,
I saw that everything was in motion.
I saw that the Halls and Palaces grew larger or smaller,
Changed their shapes and their colours.
Sometimes they fell into disuse,
Sometimes the activity in them increased.
Nothing was at rest.

THE KINGDOM OF HEAVEN

123

I sat for a while and thought over all that I had seen.

Suddenly there appeared to me — a wise old man.
He said:
You have come to the place where you must sacrifice the
    last Symbol —
Yourself.

Then he disappeared.

124

This is a thing which I cannot explain:
But I went down the further side of that mountain,
Leaving myself behind.

125

At the foot of the mountain I came to a vast open space,
Called Freedom.

For a while life seemed to be blank and empty;
And, having no motives or desires,
I was at a loss to know what to do.

Then, in the midst of the space, I saw a little tent,
Which I knew to be
The House of God.

II
GOD

GOD

ETERNAL Being:
Whose home has seldom yet been found;
Whose buff-robed, black-robed, feathered priests
Listen for word of Thee,
And, having listened,
Pour forth a babel of conflicting sound;
Who givest piteous sorrow,
As well as heavenly peace;
Who createst utter darkness,
As well as blinding light;
Whose silence — is the silence of men's hearts:

Speak — through my heart — to me.

GOD

1

God said:
You have heard all that has been told of Me;
How that I created everything and rule everything and am
 everything;
Infinite — Eternal.

You have heard how that long ago I brought the Israelites
 up from Egypt;
How that I forced the great snake Wob to come out of
 his hole in the rock;
How that I gave rain, last year,
In Sind.

2

You have heard of the idolatry, the noble deeds, done in
 My name;
The tortures, cruelties, and persecutions.

How that parents confided their children to My care,
Wives — their husbands,
Men — their destiny.

HEAVEN:

How that mankind brought their dead to Me,
Their marriages and manhoods;
And laid their griefs upon Me,
Their crimes and hopes and fears.

3

THERE is no end to the stories that have been told of Me,
No end to the list of My attributes.

Some ages made Me cruel — jealous;
Some — kind and loving.
Some sought to propitiate Me with sacrifice;
Some bade Me sacrifice Myself.

I have been prayed to take sides in war,
To heal the sick,
To change the weather,
To undo the work of My own hands.

There is no use that has not been made of Me;
No cause — which has not been given My blessing;
No land — where My pestilence and famine
Have not come.

4

You have read how that every imaginable obscenity has
  been committed in My service;
And that no abomination that ever illuminated the mind of
  man has been too low for an oblation to Me;

GOD

How that men have not hesitated to fight and to destroy,
In order to enforce their belief that their own idea of Me
Was the one true God.

5

You have seen the offerings that men have laid at My feet,
The Temples they have built;
And you have stood in reverence before the works of art
Which My name has evoked.

6

You also have worshipped Me.
You have tarried awhile in the cloisters on My mountain;
And, at the dawn, cast marigolds upon My sacred river.
You have struck the gong that speaks My name;
And in My cathedrals you have sung
My praise.

7

FOR I too am a Symbol.
The Symbol of all that men cannot understand,
Of all they can or will not do;
Of all that their hearts have longed for,
Of every happiness of which they ever dreamed.

The Symbol of power and of goodness;
Of Love and of Truth.

8

But I am more than this.
I live in all things,
I am in every man;
And the day will come when every man
Shall know Me.

9

Then will man be his own master;
Then will he link his sorrows to his own thoughts, words,
    and acts;
Then will he answer to himself for what he himself does,
And create his joys in the light of his own understanding.

10

And I shall come to reign upon this Earth of Mine;
Not one of Me, but many;
Not in one man, or a few,
But in all who know Me.

And I shall have as many thrones
As there are hearts of men.

11

At last God said:
Look, and I will show you the making of worlds.

12

AND immediately I stood where Time is not;
Where beginnings and endings are held within each other;
Where Truth exists for ever.

The everlasting outpouring and indrawing of Life,
Shining within me and without me,
In endless Being.

13

THEN — alone — I came to a river,
Where I embarked in a boat.

14

AND in a little while the river carried me under a dark archway,
Into another State.

There I climbed out of the boat
On to the Plain of Existence,
Which is also called:
Eternal Life.

III
ETERNAL LIFE

ETERNAL LIFE

Here I create;
Here I behold the meanings;
Here I catch the rhythm of life.

Here I put thoughts into words;
Words that destroy,
Words that beget.

So does the Unseen World
Come into Being.

ETERNAL LIFE

1

On the Plain of Existence,
Which is also called Eternal Life,
There were three cities.
I visited each in turn.

2

The first was the City of Creation,
Where every form of expression flourished.

The lowest building was eight thousand storeys high;
And everywhere I went, I saw signs of production,
Ever increasing production.

A large part of the city was given over to factories,
Where people made things to sell;
And advertisements urging people to buy extended over
    the outsides and insides
Of every building.

HEAVEN:

3

In one ward of the city,
Under the direction of a Dictator,
Backed by the blessings of the Church,
The citizens were having as many babies as possible;
For no particular reason.

While in another ward, there was a man being worshipped
    because he made a million motor-cars a minute;
For no particular reason.

And in a packed cathedral I heard sung a lovely hymn,
The last line of every verse of which was:
More and more and more.

4

In an open space, in the centre of the city, I watched an
    enormous crowd round a statue of Multiplication,
Which had just given birth to the idea that:
The more, the better.

By the light of it
War became more men, more munitions, more money;
And industry became more and more and more of any-
    thing that one happened to make;
And salesmanship became more and better;
And everything seemed well, so long as it only grew more
And multiplied.

5

I DID not stay long in the city;
For, to tell the truth, I was overcome by the noise and the traffic;
The deluge of books and of pictures;
The newspapers and manufactures and art.

6

BUT before I left,
An ardent apostle of progress gave me a copy of the hymn which I had heard sung.
I reproduce it here:

7

HYMN

O GOD through whom all blessings flow,
From Thy unending store
Pour down upon us here below
More and more and more.

Who taught us to invent machines,
Ten million times ten score;
Help us produce by modern means
More and more and more.

Who gavest fish and bread and meat
And fruit and herbs galore;
Grant us the appetite to eat
More and more and more.

HEAVEN:

    Who made our Empire very large,
    Stretching from shore to shore;
    Add to the peoples in our charge
    More and more and more.

    Who brought us to a vast increase
    Of frightfulness in war;
    Prepare us during times of peace,
    More and more and more.

    Who leadest unto forms of art,
    Unknown on Earth before;
    Help us create in ways that start-
    Le more and more and more.

    Augment the knowledge in our minds,
    Our science and our lore.
    Add to our learning of all kinds,
    More and more and more.

    Improve facilities for trade,
    Make all the world a store,
    And swell the profits to be made,
    More and more and more.

pp And when we pass to meet our King,
    With untold happiness,
mf Let those who follow after sing,
ff   More and more and more.

    Amen.

8

The second city was called the City of Understanding.
In it everything had a meaning;
Even a look — had a deep significance.

There I saw the meaning of ugliness, of sickness and of
 death;
The meaning of health and beauty,
Of work and idleness and tears.

9

There a house was a house,
A place for people to live in and find shelter;
Nor did it seem to matter
Whether it was ten storeys high or one,
Whether it was made of marble, or brick, or straw, or
 wood, or paper,
So long as people could live in it
And have the shelter they required.

Nor did it seem to matter what folk wore,
Or if they wore anything at all,
So long as their clothing meant to them
Comfort and beauty.

10

Of the people that I met there,
Everyone's life had a meaning;
Nor did they utter any meaningless thing.

HEAVEN:

Once even, when in a moment of forgetfulness
I began to sing that hymn which I had heard in the City
    of Creation —
More and more and more —
A number of persons asked me what it meant.

They must have thought me very stupid,
For I could only explain that it meant multiplication;
Which they said they had learned to understand
When they were very young.

11

In the centre of the city was a Science Institute,
Where I was shown the Intrinsic Meanings.

There I saw the purport of symbols, churches, classes;
The lower feeling the need of guidance and protection,
The upper feeling the need to dominate and rule.

There the inner meanings were unfolded;
There things, trees, children, happenings,
Spoke out a new significance;
So that I saw reflected in them
The meaning of myself.

12

In the laboratory of the Institute there was a great variety
    of growing cultures, at every stage of development.

ETERNAL LIFE

And I noticed that as each culture grew in extent and power,
Its meaning, which lay at the heart of it,
Grew less.
So that at last each culture outgrew its own purport,
And collapsed.
But not before it had seeded.

And from the seeds of every culture
New cultures grew up.

13

IN a storehouse in the Institute
I saw, bottled up, in huge metal cylinders,
The vast forces required before the first glimmerings of meaning
Could penetrate the skull of man.

How that it needed wars of unparalleled violence
Before he began to perceive that the mere externals of civilization
Were but the clothes of his own inner soul.

How that it required a thousand people to be killed every day
Before he began to have the smallest idea that mere movement through space in an automobile
Might mean less to creative life
Than staying still.

And how whole races had to pass their old age in chronic sickness
Before the sanctity of a body
Could come to mean as much as a profit
In drugs or groceries.

14

In the storehouse office I was shown a number of films which portrayed the astonishing results
Of the absorption of even the smallest quantity of these forces,
By a person incapable of assimilating their inner significance.

How that a man who had had a whiff of violence
Went round the world shrieking:
No more war;

And a policeman with a tender heart
Made endless new traffic regulations.

How that several diseased persons
Blossomed into ardent food-reformers;

And communism grew into a burning reality.

And how that a few drops of human love set loose
Resulted in pornography
Of a very high order.

15

Near by, in the middle of an open space, was a blaze of light,
Called Truth.

It amused me to watch the effect which it had on passers-by;
For the light was so dazzling that few, even of the inhabitants of the City of Understanding, could look upon it.
And everyone that came near felt Truth differently, depending upon how it was reflected
In his own heart.

To some it seemed one thing, to some — another;
But the light itself did not change.

16

It was a custom in the city that whenever one of the citizens was doubtful about anything,
He brought it out and looked at it in the light of Truth.
After which he was able to understand and accept it.

And it was remarkable what things were accepted there.

17

There was an interesting old house in the city,
Divided into numberless rooms and compartments,
With many stairways leading upwards and downwards.

And though the meanings of facts and experiences
Varied with the different rooms,
And depended to some extent upon whatever part of the
 building one happened to be in;
Yet all the meanings in the building were true
In relation to their environment.

And when I looked out of the window of that house,
Over the Plain of Existence,
I saw how it was possible to give a meaning to life.

18

YET I was glad to get out of the City of Understanding,
For if you will imagine to yourself how it would feel to be
 surrounded by people whose every action had signifi
 cance,
You will realize how tiresome such a situation might
 become;
And how one would long for the society of those whose
 lives followed a true intuition,
Without analysis of what each happening meant.

19

OUTSIDE I saw a crowd of people who could not understand.
Widows and parents — who could not understand why their
 husbands and children had been killed in war;
Labourers — who could not understand why their lives
 should be a drudgery and a slavery;

ETERNAL LIFE

Coloured folk — who could not understand why they should be treated as dirt.

And I noticed that, while some of them were trying to enter the city,
There were others who accepted even the hardest things,
With a blind unquestioning faith.

The resigned and simple of the Earth.

20

The city called Rhythm was the hardest to get into.
It was built upon a rock, surrounded by a ravine, over which there were few bridges.

And the city itself was in constant motion.
Up and down and round it went,
So that often the end of a bridge was in the air;
And sometimes, when I thought to enter the city,
I found myself facing a blank wall.

At last, helped by faith,
And with a certain amount of good judgment on my own part,
I stepped safely across.

21

In the city everything that was in accord with the rhythm of the moment
Went marvellously well.

Thus — if the inhabitants happened to be thinking of Sunday Morning Talks,
And one of their number felt like giving
Sunday Morning Talks,
A big business was done.

And if sewing-machines were the order of the day,
And a man found a way of making cheap sewing-machines,
Enormous numbers were produced.

While those who foresaw a future need
Made ready to launch forth at the right moment
On its fulfilment;
With great advantage to themselves.

22

While I was in the city,
Someone whispered:
Better and Brighter Service.
Which phrase appealed alike to the satisfaction of the served
As to the pride of the servants.
With the result that everywhere there was
Better and Brighter Service.

23

Only it happened that sometimes a motion was started
Which accorded with the rhythm of one half of the city
And discorded with the other half.

ETERNAL LIFE

For example: on one occasion, as I heard,
Someone had said:
No more Drink.
And all the old ladies of the city echoed:
No more Drink.
Which echo reached the Government
(Being largely composed of old ladies),
Who passed a Law — ordering:
No more Drink.

But the young men of the city,
As well as some of the old,
Were accustomed to drink;
So that they could not hear the echo.

24

THE result of it all was
That, for the time being, the question as to whether a
    grown man could drink a glass of wine in the city be-
    came a matter of such importance
That many were slain in the discussion;
And still more were put in prison.

And matters would have remained in a sad state
Had it not been that some experienced elder
Hurried off to the City of Understanding
And brought back a Grain of Sense;
Which he presented to his fellow-citizens.

So restoring them
To a more reasonable frame of mind.

25

I NOTICED that some of the inhabitants
Were not so sensitive to changes of rhythm
As others.
For which reason it was customary that certain should be
 recognized as leaders of fashion.
A custom which caused me some discomfort;
For, as a visitor, I was accorded a measure of deference
In this respect.

Thus, once, when in the street,
Thinking of that hymn which I had heard in the City of
 Creation,
I smiled to myself;
Everyone else
Smiled to himself.

In my embarrassment I hastened out of sight;
And — happily enough —
Everyone else
Hastened out of sight.

Yet the system had its advantages,
As the following story will show:

ETERNAL LIFE

26

At one time, before I came to the City of Rhythm, it was the fashion to eat in a blue coat
And Pure Purple tie.
In fact, no one would eat anything unless he had on a blue coat
And Pure Purple tie.

And it happened, so I was told, that this fashion brought the city to the verge of a great disaster;
Because the supply of Pure Purple dye ran out.
And many of the people starved,
Might even have died,
Had it not been for the noble example
Of those in high quarters.

For the beloved King of the city himself
(Who at that time was not considered to be a leader of fashions in clothes)
Had, with great forethought, and with no little pain,
Dined in public in a blue coat
And Near Purple tie.
Thus putting an end
To an intolerable situation.

And all that evening,
At dinner-time,
The bells of the city rang out in joyful peals.
Not — as was stated officially —

To mark the happiness of the people;
But — as I heard confidentially —
To drown the effect
Of that appalling discord.

27

YET, putting all these light criticisms aside,
There was abroad in the City of Rhythm
Such a sense of the fitness of things,
Such a sensitiveness to the trials and changes of life,
As I did not meet with before or since.

And even if sometimes the inhabitants came near to misfortune,
There was always forthcoming someone with sufficient right feeling
To save them from disaster.

In proof of which I will describe an incident,
Which might easily have been a painful one,
And which took place in my presence.

28

IT was the day on which the Lord Mayor of the City of Creation
Was being presented with the Freedom of the City of Rhythm.

ETERNAL LIFE

I had a seat on the platform; and I could not help remarking the magnificence of the casket containing the parchment, customary on these occasions.

On the casket were engraved the Arms of the City of Rhythm.
The crest — a Wave:
Emblazoned on the shield —
A round Peg, and a round Hole:
With a motto, in some long-forgotten language,
Which was understood to mean:
The Right Thing at the Right Moment.

At that moment occurred the incident to which I have referred.

29

THE Lord Mayor of the City of Creation rose to return thanks.

He said:
While I have been listening to the beautiful speeches,
I have been admiring this very beautiful box.
And I have been working out in my mind
A new and not expensive method
Of turning out similar beautiful boxes,
At the rate of a Hundred a Minute.

The Lord Mayor paused for approval.

During the moment of silence that followed,
The Lord Mayor corrected himself — saying:
Two Hundred a Minute.

And immediately there burst forth such a storm of appreciation as had never been known before in the City of Rhythm.
Following which, as by some happy inspiration,
The City Band struck up
The Hymn of Creation.

30

YET I heard afterwards that it had been a near thing;
And that the applause had been started by a total stranger.
No less a person than the Ambassador of the City of Understanding;
Who, realizing that the Lord Mayor of the City of Creation, in thus exalting his own ingenuity, was paying an unconscious tribute to the importance of a memorable occasion,
Had begun to clap his hands.
A proceeding which was naturally followed
By all present.

So saving the honour of the inhabitants of the City of Rhythm.

31

As for the conductor of the band,
He had not heard the speech at all.

ETERNAL LIFE

But, having already played the Hymn of Creation five
    times that morning,
He took the applause for a signal
To play it once again.

That night, when the guests had departed,
He was decorated with the Order of the Endless Wave;
For having added to the glory of the City,
Whose motto is:
The Right Thing at the Right Moment.

32

When I had come out from the three Cities,
I sat and pondered over all that I had seen.

And it seemed to me that though many creative acts had
    rhythm,
They lacked meaning;
And so led to no good result.

And if some had meaning,
They lacked rhythm;
And so were without effect.

While those actions that had both rhythm and meaning
Were few,
And very far between.

And I saw that if anyone, having understanding in his
    heart,

Could act in concert with the rhythm of life,
All the Powers of Heaven were in his grasp.

33

WHILE I was thus thinking,
I fell asleep.
And I dreamed a dream.

34

I DREAMT that I was myself able to create whatever I desired.
And into my hands there flowed all the materials and means that were needed for my work;
There was nothing that did not come to my aid.
And I dreamt that I created a new Heaven
And a new Earth.

35

AND I built:
Not Empires that would fall,
Not Armies that would perish,
Not Enthusiasms that would die out,
Not Theories that would be disproved,
Not Institutions whose use would fade,

But happy, understanding Life.

36

I BUILT new cities.
Cities which were the best in arrangement that a free intelligence could devise;
Instead of being the incoherent growths of economic laws.

Cities which were designed with the artistry of meaning;
Instead of following the conventions of outworn opinion.

I built them in my dream.

37

AND I peopled them with men and women,
Free men — creators.

Not with fettered, tradition-tied puppets,
But with livers of Eternal Life.

Not with takers-out of insurances against the wrath of God,
Or an early death;
But with men who did what they did because they knew it to be useful and genuine.

Not with hopers or watchers or waiters or knowers,
Not with frightened invalids or bewildered war-makers,
Not with followers or blind producers,
Or with mere consumers;

But with wise and fearless creators.

38

AND while I built, I destroyed.

I destroyed institutions that used their authority to stifle thought and to prevent criticism;

I destroyed individuals who considered only themselves; who defiled their bodies, and who shut out truth from their minds;

Who closed their eyes to facts,

And who worshipped their own opinions.

I destroyed them in my dream.

39

THEN I threw ridicule upon all that was false.

So that it was no longer possible for well-housed priests, however plausible,

To exhort the dwellers in slums, however stupid, to love their neighbours as themselves.

And no rich person could ever again dare to insult his God by giving to a beggar

Without at the same time being thankful for the opportunity of ridding himself of the symbol of his own selfishness.

And no sincere nation could ever again spend millions on preparing for war

While announcing that it stood for peace.

40

Then my dream changed and I began to accept all that
   happened:
To say yes to everything that ever existed.
Yes to history and to tragedy and to despair,
Yes to old men hurrying along with remedies,
Yes to young men sacrificing their lives for a cause that
   would not live a month,
Yes to heroes, yes to slaves,
Yes to everything that lived.

And I laughed.
I laughed at my fears and hopes and precautions;
Then I laughed again for joy.

Until the sound of my laughter
Woke me up.

And I felt sad that my dream
Was only a dream.

41

Suddenly there appeared once more to me
That same wise old man whom I had seen on Mount Medi-
   tation.

He said:
A long way from here there is a garden;

And in that garden lives a Being,
In whom are the faculties of Creation, of Understanding, and of Rhythm.

42

The story of my journey to that garden is written in astronomy and in geology,
And in the history of plants and of the animals and of the human race.

As to the garden,
Innumerable books have been written about it,
And about every part of it.

43

The Being who lives in the garden,
In whom are the faculties of Creation and Understanding and Rhythm,
Is man.

About the Author

Frank Townshend lived in England from 1887 to 1974. He attended the Royal Military Academy as a young man, was commissioned into the Royal Engineers in 1906, and was promoted to Lieutenant in 1908. He eventually became a Captain and served in World War I in France with the Field Army for most of the war. He was awarded the Military Cross and Croix de Chevalier in early 1916, and finally left the Army in 1926. All that is known of him beyond this is that he was an author, poet and artist who studied at Ecole
Julien in Paris, lived in India for a while, contributed articles to Theosophist and Buddhist magazines, and remained unmarried.

He wrote five books titled *Earth* (1929), *Heaven* (1930), *Becoming* (1939), *Amen* (1952) and *Hell* (1955). His books are considered amazing and life-changing for most who read them. For example, his book *Earth* inspired a choral symphony called "Vision of the Earth," and one book reviewer said, "This may be the most important book ever written about mankind and our relationship to all things. Part philosophy, part religion, part poetry, the book is an observation of mankind and how we have evolved over history into what we are and what our lives are today. No author has ever summarized humanity as correctly as Frank Townshend. It's the closest to a comprehensive understanding of the totality of existence as we can have in print." Few people know of his work, so The Book Tree is the only publisher to find his first two titles and bring them back into print. We hope to reprint them all, if found, so that his work will not be forgotten.

www.ingramcontent.com/pod-product-compliance
Lightning Source LLC
Chambersburg PA
CBHW061452040426
42450CB00007B/1333